T0199191

Her Christmas Wish

Paula M. Brown

Introducing Drawings by Kori Elise Mitchell
Illustrated by Niah Caesar

WestBow Press books may be ordered through booksellers or by contacting:

WestBow Press
A Division of Thomas Nelson & Zondervan
1663 Liberty Drive
Bloomington, IN 47403
www.westbowpress.com
844-714-3454

Scripture taken from the New King James Version® Copyright © 1982 by Thomas Nelson. Used by permission. All rights reserved.

ISBN: 978-1-6642-2407-0 (sc)
ISBN: 978-1-6642-2408-7 (e)

Library of Congress Control Number: 2021903323

Print information available on the last page.

WestBow Press rev. date: 03/08/2021

WESTBOW
P R E S S®
A DIVISION OF THOMAS NELSON
& ZONDERVAN

"For there is born to you this day
in the city of David a Savior,
Who is Christ the Lord.
And this will be a sign to you:
You will find a Babe wrapped in
swaddling cloths, in a manger."
Luke 2:11 NKJV

A young girl and her mother
Spent the day at the mall
Searching for holiday gifts
For family and friends – one and all.

Before leaving the mall,
They caught a glimpse of a sleigh.
The girl pleaded with her mother
To see Santa that day.

"Oh please, Mom, may we go?
I have one question to ask."
Her mom smiled and then nodded,
And led her straight to the task.

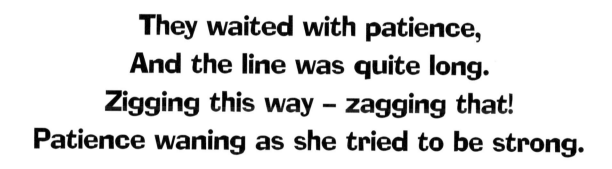

They waited with patience,
And the line was quite long.
Zigging this way – zagging that!
Patience waning as she tried to be strong.

Each child waiting to tell Santa
What they wanted this year,
including how good they've been;
I'm sure he wanted to hear.

The nearer they drew to Santa,
The more excited the young girl became.
Soon it was her turn.
Then, Santa asked her her name.

"Samantha," she said,
And she noticed his smile.
Santa asked her what she wanted.
"I have one question," she replied.

"What is Christmas really about?
Being good? Friends and family?
The gifts that we give?"
"No, Christmas is about loving others
Each day that we live.

Christmas has nothing to do with
Santa or Mrs. Claus,
Or the sleigh and reindeer.
No, that's not it at all.

Christmas is God-breathed;
God's gift of life and love.
The gift that can only come from
The Heavenly Father above.

The Lord sent His Son, Jesus,
To show us how we must live.
Be kind to one another,
And to all those who have little, we must give.

Spread joy where there is sadness;
Laughter when there is pain;
Hope when things seem hopeless;
Spread sunshine when there is rain;

Understanding when there's confusion;
Compassion when one feels blue;
When you do these things for others,
Others will do them for you too.

Be good and kind, and don't be mean.
Remember life is not always fair.
As long as you love with all your heart,
Christmas will forever be there.

This job I have brings hope to kids;
God's gift on Christmas day.
This hope was meant for everyone
Who believes what the Scriptures say.

I am proud of the job I have;
Bringing joy to kids like you.
Every day I bring smiles to their faces
And the hope for something new."

Jesus – the Hope for all mankind –
Came down from his Heavenly throne.
A star did shine that fateful night
Which led to the babe wrapped
in swaddling clothes."

"Then, that will be my Christmas wish;
To love with all my heart.
I'll make each day more like Christmas.
That sounds like a very good place to start.

I'll love the unloved without reproach,
And give to those in need.
Share joy with anyone who's sad at heart,
Shine the light of love for all to see.

I'll strive to make a difference,
In the lives of those I love,
With a kind word or gesture.
It'll be my praise to God above.

Christmas will be every day for me.
I'll live to love one and all.
The days when it gets hard for me,
On Jesus I will call."

The girl got her answer
And was puzzled no more.
She must live to love everyone.
Only the love of God can restore.

As you see your neighbor in need,
Don't turn and walk away.
Show the love you have in your heart
And do a good deed every day

Jesus sought those who moved through life
So far from the Father's heart.
That's the true reason we celebrate Christmas.
To the world, His truth we must impart.

Jesus is the true gift to us;
The reason we celebrate in this way.
Shepherds and wisemen traveled from afar
To witness His arrival on Christmas day.

Jesus Is The Reason For The Season!

Acknowledgements

Thank You:

This poem is the original work of Paula M. Brown. Any reference to any person(s) is (are) strictly based on the author's personal experiences. All materials based on the scriptures in the Holy Bible, adopted from the Gospels, and is intended for personal preference and teaching of the reader(s).

All photographs submitted were the sole ownership of the author, or with authorization of friends and family; unless otherwise noted.

The drawings were done by Kori Elise Mitchell in collaboration with the author's poem. Thank you for your submissions, and continue drawing. I look forward to seeing your work go far beyond this book, and maybe, dare I say, as far as you publishing your own drawings someday. Thank you for the part you played in getting this completed.

To everyone who stood beside me, behind me pushing me, and those who walked with me as I took this journey, I cannot thank you enough.

May God continue to bless and keep you all!

And to anyone who reads and shares this book, my prayer is that it will warm your heart and pierce your soul.

"Let, the words of my mouth and the meditation of my heart be acceptable in your sight, O Lord, my strength and my Redeemer." (Psalms 19:14)

About the Author

Paula M. Brown, though this is her first attempt at writing children's stories, has been writing poetry for many years. She self-published her first book in 2019 titled Spiritually Speaking: Poems for the Soul, which can be found on Amazonbooks.com. She tells her story of how she found God in a way children, and even adults, can relate.

Printed in the United States
by Baker & Taylor Publisher Services